50 Premium Vietnamese Dinner Recipes for Home

By: Kelly Johnson

Table of Contents

- Pho Bo (Beef Pho)
- Bun Cha (Grilled Pork with Noodles)
- Banh Xeo (Vietnamese Sizzling Pancakes)
- Ca Kho To (Caramelized Fish in Clay Pot)
- Goi Cuon (Fresh Spring Rolls)
- Bo Luc Lac (Shaking Beef)
- Bun Bo Hue (Spicy Beef Noodle Soup)
- Com tam (Broken Rice with Grilled Pork)
- Cha Ca La Vong (Turmeric Fish with Dill)
- Ga Nuong (Grilled Chicken)
- Mi Quang (Quang Style Noodles)
- Banh Mi (Vietnamese Sandwich)
- Hu Tieu (Cantonese-Style Noodle Soup)
- Goi Ga (Chicken Salad)
- Thit Kho Trung (Braised Pork and Eggs)
- Bun Thit Nuong (Grilled Pork Noodles)
- Hu Tieu Xao (Stir-Fried Noodles)
- Ca Hap (Steamed Fish)
- Cha Gio (Fried Spring Rolls)
- Xoi Ga (Sticky Rice with Chicken)
- Ga Kho Gung (Ginger Chicken)
- Mi Xao Don (Crispy Noodles)
- Bo Kho (Beef Stew)
- Bun Rieu (Crab Noodle Soup)
- Canh Chua (Sour Soup)
- Cha Lua (Vietnamese Pork Sausage)
- Rau Muong Xao (Stir-Fried Water Spinach)
- Bun Bo Nam Bo (Southern Beef Noodles)
- Pho Ga (Chicken Pho)
- Ga Kho (Caramelized Chicken)
- Canh Kho Qua (Bitter Melon Soup)
- Goi Du Du (Papaya Salad)
- Banh Cuon (Steamed Rice Rolls)
- Banh Trang Cuon Thit Heo (Rice Paper Rolls with Pork)
- Xoi Xeo (Sticky Rice with Mung Beans)

- Bo Nuong La Chanh (Grilled Beef with Lime Leaves)
- Thit Heo Kho (Braised Pork)
- Bun Oc (Snail Noodles)
- Che Ba Mau (Three-Color Dessert)
- Mi Quang with Shrimp
- Bo La Lot (Beef Wrapped in Betel Leaves)
- Banh Mi Thit Nuong (Grilled Pork Sandwich)
- Hu Tieu Mi (Mixed Noodle Soup)
- Cha Ca Thang Long (Dill Fish)
- Goi Muong (Green Mango Salad)
- Banh Bao (Vietnamese Steamed Buns)
- Thit Kho Tau (Braised Pork with Eggs)
- Bun Chay (Vegetarian Noodles)
- Ruou Vang (Vietnamese Wine Steamed Fish)
- Xoi Ga (Sticky Rice with Chicken and Mushroom)

Pho Bo (Beef Pho)

Ingredients:

- 2 lbs beef bones
- 1 lb beef brisket
- 1 onion, halved
- 1 piece of ginger, halved
- 2 star anise
- 1 cinnamon stick
- 4 cloves
- 1 tablespoon fish sauce
- 1 tablespoon salt
- Rice noodles (banh pho)
- Fresh herbs (basil, cilantro)
- Lime wedges

Instructions:

1. **Prepare the Broth**
   Boil beef bones for 5 minutes, drain, and rinse. Add bones, brisket, onion, ginger, spices, fish sauce, and salt to a large pot with 4 quarts of water. Simmer for 6 hours.
2. **Strain the Broth**
   Remove the bones and brisket. Strain the broth through a fine mesh.
3. **Cook the Noodles**
   Cook rice noodles according to package instructions.
4. **Assemble the Pho**
   Slice the brisket thinly. Serve noodles in bowls, top with beef slices, ladle hot broth over, and garnish with herbs and lime.

Bun Cha (Grilled Pork with Noodles)

Ingredients:

- 1 lb pork belly, thinly sliced
- 1/4 cup fish sauce
- 1/4 cup sugar
- 1 tablespoon minced garlic
- 1 tablespoon minced shallots
- Rice vermicelli noodles
- Fresh herbs (mint, cilantro)
- Lettuce leaves
- Carrots and daikon for pickling

Instructions:

1. **Marinate the Pork**
   Mix fish sauce, sugar, garlic, and shallots. Marinate pork for at least 1 hour.
2. **Grill the Pork**
   Grill marinated pork until cooked through and slightly charred.
3. **Prepare Noodles**
   Cook rice vermicelli noodles according to package instructions.
4. **Assemble Bun Cha**
   Serve grilled pork over noodles with fresh herbs, lettuce, and pickled vegetables.

Banh Xeo (Vietnamese Sizzling Pancakes)

Ingredients:

- 1 cup rice flour
- 1 cup coconut milk
- 1 cup water
- 1 teaspoon turmeric powder
- 1/2 lb shrimp, peeled
- 1 cup bean sprouts
- Lettuce leaves
- Fresh herbs (mint, cilantro)
- Nuoc cham (dipping sauce)

Instructions:

1. **Prepare the Batter**
   Mix rice flour, coconut milk, water, and turmeric to form a smooth batter.
2. **Cook the Pancakes**
   Heat a non-stick pan with oil, pour in batter, and add shrimp and bean sprouts. Cook until the edges are crispy.
3. **Serve**
   Fold pancakes in half and serve with lettuce leaves, fresh herbs, and dipping sauce.

Ca Kho To (Caramelized Fish in Clay Pot)

Ingredients:

- 1 lb catfish, cut into pieces
- 1/4 cup fish sauce
- 1/4 cup sugar
- 1/2 cup coconut water
- 1 onion, sliced
- 2 green onions, chopped
- Black pepper

Instructions:

1. **Caramelize Sugar**
   In a clay pot, melt sugar until golden brown.
2. **Add Ingredients**
   Add fish, fish sauce, coconut water, onion, and black pepper.
3. **Simmer**
   Cover and simmer on low heat for 20-30 minutes until fish is cooked through.
4. **Garnish and Serve**
   Top with green onions and serve with rice.

Goi Cuon (Fresh Spring Rolls)

Ingredients:

- Rice paper wrappers
- 1/2 lb shrimp, cooked and sliced
- 1 cup vermicelli noodles, cooked
- Fresh herbs (mint, cilantro, basil)
- Lettuce leaves
- Peanut sauce for dipping

Instructions:

1. **Prepare the Wrappers**
   Soak rice paper in warm water until pliable.
2. **Assemble the Rolls**
   Lay the wrapper flat, add shrimp, noodles, herbs, and lettuce. Roll tightly.
3. **Serve**
   Serve with peanut sauce for dipping.

Bo Luc Lac (Shaking Beef)

Ingredients:

- 1 lb beef tenderloin, cubed
- 2 tablespoons soy sauce
- 1 tablespoon oyster sauce
- 1 tablespoon garlic, minced
- 1 tablespoon black pepper
- 1 tablespoon vegetable oil
- Fresh herbs for garnish

Instructions:

1. **Marinate the Beef**
   Mix beef with soy sauce, oyster sauce, garlic, and black pepper. Marinate for 30 minutes.
2. **Sear the Beef**
   Heat oil in a pan, add beef, and cook until browned, shaking the pan occasionally.
3. **Serve**
   Garnish with fresh herbs and serve with rice.

Bun Bo Hue (Spicy Beef Noodle Soup)

Ingredients:

- 1 lb beef shank
- 1 lb pork hocks
- 1 onion, halved
- 2 stalks lemongrass, smashed
- 1 tablespoon chili paste
- 1 tablespoon fish sauce
- Rice noodles
- Fresh herbs and lime for garnish

Instructions:

1. **Prepare the Broth**
   In a pot, boil beef shank and pork hocks with onion and lemongrass for 1.5 hours.
2. **Strain the Broth**
   Remove meat and strain the broth.
3. **Season the Broth**
   Add chili paste and fish sauce to the broth.
4. **Serve**
   Cook rice noodles, place in bowls, add meat, ladle broth over, and garnish with herbs and lime.

Com Tam (Broken Rice with Grilled Pork)

Ingredients:

- 2 cups broken rice
- 1 lb pork chop, marinated
- 1/4 cup fish sauce
- 1 tablespoon sugar
- 1 teaspoon black pepper
- Pickled vegetables for garnish

Instructions:

1. **Cook the Rice**
   Cook broken rice according to package instructions.
2. **Grill the Pork**
   Marinate pork with fish sauce, sugar, and black pepper. Grill until cooked through.
3. **Serve**
   Plate the rice, top with grilled pork, and garnish with pickled vegetables.

Cha Ca La Vong (Turmeric Fish with Dill)

Ingredients:

- 1 lb fish fillets (catfish or tilapia)
- 1/4 cup turmeric powder
- 1/4 cup fish sauce
- 2 tablespoons vegetable oil
- 1 bunch dill, chopped
- 2 green onions, chopped
- Rice noodles
- Peanuts for garnish

Instructions:

1. **Marinate the Fish**
   Combine turmeric, fish sauce, and oil. Marinate fish fillets for at least 30 minutes.
2. **Cook the Fish**
   Heat a skillet over medium heat, add the marinated fish, and cook until golden brown.
3. **Serve**
   Serve fish over rice noodles, topped with dill, green onions, and peanuts.

Ga Nuong (Grilled Chicken)

Ingredients:

- 1 whole chicken, spatchcocked
- 1/4 cup fish sauce
- 2 tablespoons sugar
- 2 tablespoons garlic, minced
- 1 tablespoon black pepper
- Lime wedges for serving

Instructions:

1. **Marinate the Chicken**
   Mix fish sauce, sugar, garlic, and black pepper. Marinate chicken for at least 2 hours.
2. **Grill the Chicken**
   Preheat grill to medium heat. Grill chicken for about 40 minutes, flipping occasionally.
3. **Serve**
   Serve with lime wedges on the side.

Mi Quang (Quang Style Noodles)

Ingredients:

- 8 oz rice noodles
- 1/2 lb shrimp, peeled
- 1/2 lb pork belly, sliced
- 4 cups broth (chicken or pork)
- 2 tablespoons fish sauce
- Fresh herbs (mint, cilantro)
- Peanuts for garnish

Instructions:

1. **Cook the Noodles**
   Cook rice noodles according to package instructions and set aside.
2. **Prepare the Broth**
   In a pot, simmer pork belly and shrimp in broth with fish sauce until cooked through.
3. **Serve**
   Place noodles in bowls, ladle broth over, and garnish with herbs and peanuts.

Banh Mi (Vietnamese Sandwich)

Ingredients:

- Baguette
- 1/2 lb grilled pork or chicken
- Pickled carrots and daikon
- Fresh cucumber slices
- Cilantro sprigs
- Sriracha or mayonnaise

Instructions:

1. **Prepare the Baguette**
   Slice baguette in half, lightly toast if desired.
2. **Assemble the Sandwich**
   Layer grilled meat, pickled vegetables, cucumber, and cilantro in the baguette.
3. **Add Sauce**
   Drizzle with Sriracha or spread mayonnaise before serving.

Hu Tieu (Cantonese-Style Noodle Soup)

Ingredients:

- 8 oz rice noodles
- 1/2 lb shrimp, peeled
- 1/2 lb pork, sliced
- 4 cups pork broth
- 2 tablespoons fish sauce
- Green onions and cilantro for garnish

Instructions:

1. **Cook the Noodles**
   Cook rice noodles according to package instructions and set aside.
2. **Prepare the Soup**
   In a pot, bring broth to a boil, add pork and shrimp, and cook until done.
3. **Serve**
   Place noodles in bowls, ladle soup over, and garnish with green onions and cilantro.

Goi Ga (Chicken Salad)

Ingredients:

- 2 cups cooked chicken, shredded
- 1/2 cup cabbage, shredded
- 1/2 cup carrots, shredded
- 1/4 cup mint leaves, chopped
- 1/4 cup fish sauce
- 1 tablespoon sugar
- Lime juice to taste

Instructions:

1. **Mix the Salad**
   In a bowl, combine chicken, cabbage, carrots, and mint.
2. **Prepare the Dressing**
   Whisk together fish sauce, sugar, and lime juice.
3. **Combine and Serve**
   Pour dressing over the salad, mix well, and serve chilled.

Thit Kho Trung (Braised Pork and Eggs)

Ingredients:

- 1 lb pork belly, cut into cubes
- 4 hard-boiled eggs
- 1/4 cup fish sauce
- 1/4 cup sugar
- 1 cup coconut water
- Black pepper to taste

Instructions:

1. **Brown the Pork**
   In a pot, caramelize sugar until golden, add pork, and brown on all sides.
2. **Add Ingredients**
   Add fish sauce, coconut water, and pepper. Simmer for 30 minutes.
3. **Add Eggs**
   Add hard-boiled eggs and cook for an additional 15 minutes.
4. **Serve**
   Serve with rice.

Bun Thit Nuong (Grilled Pork Noodles)

Ingredients:

- 8 oz rice vermicelli noodles
- 1 lb pork shoulder, thinly sliced
- 1/4 cup fish sauce
- 1/4 cup sugar
- Fresh herbs (mint, cilantro)
- Crushed peanuts for garnish

Instructions:

1. **Marinate the Pork**
   Mix fish sauce and sugar. Marinate pork for at least 1 hour.
2. **Grill the Pork**
   Grill marinated pork until cooked through and slightly charred.
3. **Prepare Noodles**
   Cook rice vermicelli noodles according to package instructions.
4. **Serve**
   Serve noodles topped with grilled pork, fresh herbs, and crushed peanuts.

Hu Tieu Xao (Stir-Fried Noodles)

Ingredients:

- 8 oz rice noodles
- 1/2 lb shrimp, peeled
- 1/2 lb pork, thinly sliced
- 1 cup mixed vegetables (carrots, bell peppers, bean sprouts)
- 3 tablespoons soy sauce
- 2 tablespoons oyster sauce
- 1 tablespoon vegetable oil
- Green onions for garnish

Instructions:

1. **Cook the Noodles**
   Prepare rice noodles according to package instructions and drain.
2. **Stir-Fry the Meat**
   In a wok, heat oil over medium-high heat. Add pork and shrimp, stir-frying until cooked through.
3. **Add Vegetables and Sauces**
   Add mixed vegetables, soy sauce, and oyster sauce. Stir-fry for another 2-3 minutes.
4. **Combine with Noodles**
   Add the cooked noodles, tossing to combine. Serve hot, garnished with green onions.

Ca Hap (Steamed Fish)

Ingredients:

- 1 whole fish (snapper or tilapia)
- 2 tablespoons fish sauce
- 1 tablespoon ginger, sliced
- 2 green onions, chopped
- 1 tablespoon cilantro, chopped
- Lime wedges for serving

Instructions:

1. **Prepare the Fish**
   Clean and score the fish, then place in a steaming dish.
2. **Add Seasonings**
   Drizzle fish sauce over the fish and top with ginger and green onions.
3. **Steam the Fish**
   Steam for about 15-20 minutes, or until the fish is cooked through.
4. **Serve**
   Serve hot with cilantro and lime wedges.

Cha Gio (Fried Spring Rolls)

Ingredients:

- 8 rice paper wrappers
- 1/2 lb ground pork
- 1/4 cup carrots, julienned
- 1/4 cup mushrooms, chopped
- 1/4 cup vermicelli noodles, soaked and chopped
- 1 egg, beaten
- Vegetable oil for frying

Instructions:

1. **Prepare the Filling**
   In a bowl, mix ground pork, carrots, mushrooms, vermicelli, and half the egg.
2. **Wrap the Spring Rolls**
   Soak rice paper in warm water until soft. Place a spoonful of filling on the wrapper, roll tightly, and seal the edges.
3. **Fry the Spring Rolls**
   Heat oil in a pan over medium heat. Fry spring rolls until golden brown and crispy.
4. **Serve**
   Serve hot with dipping sauce.

Xoi Ga (Sticky Rice with Chicken)

Ingredients:

- 2 cups sticky rice
- 1/2 lb chicken thighs
- 2 tablespoons soy sauce
- 1 tablespoon oyster sauce
- 1 tablespoon vegetable oil
- Fried shallots for garnish

Instructions:

1. **Prepare the Rice**
   Soak sticky rice in water for at least 4 hours, then steam until cooked.
2. **Cook the Chicken**
   In a pan, heat oil over medium heat. Add chicken, soy sauce, and oyster sauce. Cook until chicken is done, then shred.
3. **Serve**
   Serve sticky rice topped with shredded chicken and fried shallots.

Ga Kho Gung (Ginger Chicken)

Ingredients:

- 1 lb chicken, cut into pieces
- 1/4 cup fish sauce
- 2 tablespoons sugar
- 1/4 cup ginger, sliced
- 1 tablespoon vegetable oil
- Black pepper to taste

Instructions:

1. **Marinate the Chicken**
   Mix chicken with fish sauce, sugar, ginger, and black pepper. Marinate for at least 30 minutes.
2. **Cook the Chicken**
   In a pot, heat oil over medium heat. Add marinated chicken and cook until browned.
3. **Simmer**
   Add a little water and simmer until chicken is tender.
4. **Serve**
   Serve hot with rice.

Mi Xao Don (Crispy Noodles)

Ingredients:

- 8 oz egg noodles
- 1/2 lb shrimp, peeled
- 1/2 lb chicken, sliced
- 1 cup mixed vegetables (bell peppers, carrots, peas)
- 2 tablespoons soy sauce
- 1 tablespoon oyster sauce
- Vegetable oil for frying

Instructions:

1. **Cook the Noodles**
   Boil egg noodles according to package instructions and drain.
2. **Fry the Noodles**
   Heat oil in a pan. Add noodles in a flat layer and fry until crispy. Flip and fry the other side. Remove and drain on paper towels.
3. **Stir-Fry the Meat and Vegetables**
   In the same pan, stir-fry shrimp, chicken, and vegetables with soy sauce and oyster sauce until cooked.
4. **Serve**
   Place the crispy noodles on a plate, top with stir-fried mixture, and serve.

Bo Kho (Beef Stew)

Ingredients:

- 2 lbs beef chuck, cut into cubes
- 1 onion, chopped
- 2 carrots, sliced
- 1 tablespoon ginger, minced
- 1/4 cup fish sauce
- 2 tablespoons sugar
- 4 cups beef broth
- Fresh herbs for garnish

Instructions:

1. **Brown the Beef**
   In a pot, brown beef cubes over medium heat, then remove.
2. **Cook the Vegetables**
   Add onion and ginger to the pot, cooking until fragrant.
3. **Add Remaining Ingredients**
   Return beef to pot with carrots, fish sauce, sugar, and beef broth. Simmer for 1.5 to 2 hours until beef is tender.
4. **Serve**
   Serve hot, garnished with fresh herbs.

Bun Rieu (Crab Noodle Soup)

Ingredients:

- 8 oz rice vermicelli noodles
- 1/2 lb crab meat
- 4 cups broth (chicken or pork)
- 2 tomatoes, chopped
- 1/4 cup fish sauce
- Fresh herbs (basil, mint)
- Lime wedges for serving

Instructions:

1. **Cook the Noodles**
   Prepare rice vermicelli according to package instructions and set aside.
2. **Prepare the Broth**
   In a pot, combine broth, tomatoes, and fish sauce. Bring to a boil.
3. **Add Crab Meat**
   Stir in crab meat and simmer for 10 minutes.
4. **Serve**
   Place noodles in bowls, ladle broth over, and garnish with herbs and lime wedges.

Canh Chua (Sour Soup)

Ingredients:

- 1 lb fish (catfish or tilapia)
- 4 cups water
- 2 tomatoes, quartered
- 1 cup pineapple, chopped
- 1 cup bean sprouts
- 2 tablespoons tamarind paste
- 2 tablespoons fish sauce
- Fresh herbs (basil, cilantro) for garnish
- Chili peppers for serving

Instructions:

1. **Prepare the Broth**
   In a pot, bring water to a boil. Add tamarind paste, fish sauce, tomatoes, and pineapple.
2. **Cook the Fish**
   Add fish and simmer for 10-15 minutes until cooked through.
3. **Add Vegetables**
   Stir in bean sprouts and cook for another 2-3 minutes.
4. **Serve**
   Garnish with fresh herbs and chili peppers. Serve hot.

Cha Lua (Vietnamese Pork Sausage)

Ingredients:

- 1 lb ground pork
- 1 tablespoon fish sauce
- 1 tablespoon sugar
- 1 teaspoon pepper
- 1 tablespoon tapioca starch
- Banana leaves for wrapping

Instructions:

1. **Mix Ingredients**
   In a bowl, combine ground pork, fish sauce, sugar, pepper, and tapioca starch until well mixed.
2. **Wrap the Mixture**
   Spoon the mixture onto banana leaves, roll tightly, and secure with twine.
3. **Steam**
   Steam for about 30-40 minutes until cooked through.
4. **Serve**
   Slice and serve with dipping sauce or as part of a meal.

Rau Muong Xao (Stir-Fried Water Spinach)

Ingredients:

- 1 lb water spinach (rau muong)
- 3 cloves garlic, minced
- 1 tablespoon oyster sauce
- 1 tablespoon fish sauce
- 1 tablespoon vegetable oil

Instructions:

1. **Prepare the Vegetables**
   Wash and cut water spinach into manageable lengths.
2. **Stir-Fry**
   Heat oil in a pan over medium heat. Add garlic and sauté until fragrant.
3. **Add Water Spinach**
   Add water spinach, oyster sauce, and fish sauce. Stir-fry until wilted, about 3-5 minutes.
4. **Serve**
   Serve hot as a side dish.

Bun Bo Nam Bo (Southern Beef Noodles)

Ingredients:

- 8 oz rice vermicelli noodles
- 1 lb beef, thinly sliced
- 1/4 cup fish sauce
- 2 tablespoons sugar
- 1 tablespoon lime juice
- Fresh herbs (basil, mint)
- Crushed peanuts for garnish
- Fried shallots for garnish

Instructions:

1. **Cook the Noodles**
   Prepare rice vermicelli according to package instructions and drain.
2. **Cook the Beef**
   In a pan, cook sliced beef with fish sauce and sugar until done.
3. **Assemble the Dish**
   Place noodles in a bowl, top with beef, fresh herbs, and crushed peanuts.
4. **Serve**
   Drizzle with lime juice and garnish with fried shallots.

Pho Ga (Chicken Pho)

Ingredients:

- 8 oz rice noodles
- 1 whole chicken
- 8 cups chicken broth
- 1 onion, halved
- 1 piece ginger, sliced
- 2 tablespoons fish sauce
- Fresh herbs (basil, cilantro)
- Lime wedges for serving

Instructions:

1. **Prepare the Broth**
   In a pot, combine chicken, broth, onion, ginger, and fish sauce. Bring to a boil and simmer for 30-40 minutes.
2. **Cook the Noodles**
   Prepare rice noodles according to package instructions.
3. **Shred the Chicken**
   Remove chicken from the pot, shred, and set aside.
4. **Assemble the Dish**
   Place noodles in bowls, top with shredded chicken and ladle over broth. Garnish with fresh herbs and lime wedges.

Ga Kho (Caramelized Chicken)

Ingredients:

- 1 lb chicken thighs, cut into pieces
- 1/4 cup fish sauce
- 1/4 cup sugar
- 1 onion, chopped
- 2 cloves garlic, minced
- 1 tablespoon vegetable oil
- Black pepper to taste

Instructions:

1. **Caramelize Sugar**
   In a pot, heat sugar over medium heat until it melts and turns golden.
2. **Add Chicken**
   Add chicken, fish sauce, onion, garlic, and pepper. Cook until chicken is browned.
3. **Simmer**
   Add water to cover chicken and simmer for about 30 minutes until tender.
4. **Serve**
   Serve hot with rice.

Canh Kho Qua (Bitter Melon Soup)

Ingredients:

- 2 bitter melons, sliced
- 4 cups chicken or pork broth
- 1/2 lb ground pork
- 1 onion, chopped
- 2 cloves garlic, minced
- 2 tablespoons fish sauce
- Fresh herbs for garnish

Instructions:

1. **Prepare the Broth**
   In a pot, combine broth, onion, and garlic. Bring to a boil.
2. **Add Bitter Melon**
   Add sliced bitter melon and cook for about 5 minutes.
3. **Add Ground Pork**
   Form small meatballs with ground pork and add to the pot. Cook until meat is done.
4. **Serve**
   Garnish with fresh herbs and serve hot.

Goi Du Du (Papaya Salad)

Ingredients:

- 2 cups green papaya, shredded
- 1/2 cup carrots, shredded
- 1/4 cup peanuts, crushed
- 2 tablespoons fish sauce
- 1 tablespoon lime juice
- 1 tablespoon sugar
- Fresh herbs (cilantro, mint)

Instructions:

1. **Mix the Dressing**
   In a bowl, whisk together fish sauce, lime juice, and sugar.
2. **Combine Salad Ingredients**
   In a large bowl, combine shredded papaya, carrots, and dressing. Toss to combine.
3. **Serve**
   Top with crushed peanuts and fresh herbs. Serve chilled.

Banh Cuon (Steamed Rice Rolls)

Ingredients:

- 1 cup rice flour
- 1/2 cup tapioca flour
- 2 cups water
- 1/2 lb ground pork
- 1/2 cup minced mushrooms
- 1 onion, chopped
- Fish sauce for seasoning
- Fresh herbs for serving

Instructions:

1. **Prepare the Batter**
   In a bowl, mix rice flour, tapioca flour, and water until smooth.
2. **Cook the Filling**
   In a pan, sauté onion, add ground pork, mushrooms, and season with fish sauce. Cook until done.
3. **Steam the Rolls**
   Grease a flat dish and pour a thin layer of batter. Steam for about 5 minutes until set.
4. **Assemble the Rolls**
   Remove from the steamer, fill with pork mixture, and roll up. Serve with herbs and dipping sauce.

Banh Trang Cuon Thit Heo (Rice Paper Rolls with Pork)

Ingredients:

- 8 rice paper wrappers
- 1 lb pork belly, boiled and sliced
- 1 cup vermicelli noodles, cooked
- Fresh herbs (mint, cilantro)
- Lettuce leaves
- Hoisin sauce for dipping

Instructions:

1. **Prepare the Ingredients**
   Lay out rice paper wrappers. Arrange pork, noodles, lettuce, and herbs in the center.
2. **Roll the Wrappers**
   Dip rice paper in warm water until softened. Place filling and roll tightly.
3. **Serve**
   Serve with hoisin sauce for dipping.

Xoi Xeo (Sticky Rice with Mung Beans)

Ingredients:

- 2 cups glutinous rice
- 1 cup mung beans, soaked
- 1 tablespoon salt
- 1 tablespoon oil
- Fried shallots for garnish

Instructions:

1. **Prepare the Rice and Beans**
   Soak glutinous rice and mung beans overnight. Drain.
2. **Steam the Mixture**
   In a steamer, layer mung beans and glutinous rice. Steam for about 30 minutes.
3. **Season**
   Mix with salt and oil.
4. **Serve**
   Garnish with fried shallots and serve warm.

Bo Nuong La Chanh (Grilled Beef with Lime Leaves)

Ingredients:

- 1 lb beef, thinly sliced
- 1/4 cup lime leaves, finely chopped
- 2 tablespoons fish sauce
- 2 tablespoons sugar
- Black pepper to taste

Instructions:

1. **Marinate the Beef**
   Combine beef, lime leaves, fish sauce, sugar, and pepper. Marinate for at least 30 minutes.
2. **Grill the Beef**
   Grill on medium heat until cooked through, about 2-3 minutes per side.
3. **Serve**
   Serve hot with rice or as a filling for rice paper rolls.

Thit Heo Kho (Braised Pork)

Ingredients:

- 1 lb pork belly, cut into chunks
- 1/4 cup fish sauce
- 1/4 cup sugar
- 1 onion, sliced
- 2 cloves garlic, minced
- 2 cups coconut water

Instructions:

1. **Sear the Pork**
   In a pot, brown pork belly over medium heat.
2. **Add Ingredients**
   Add onion, garlic, fish sauce, sugar, and coconut water.
3. **Simmer**
   Cover and simmer for 40 minutes until tender.
4. **Serve**
   Serve with rice.

Bun Oc (Snail Noodles)

Ingredients:

- 8 oz rice vermicelli noodles
- 1 lb snails, cleaned
- 4 cups chicken or pork broth
- 2 tomatoes, chopped
- Fish sauce to taste
- Fresh herbs for garnish

Instructions:

1. **Cook the Broth**
   In a pot, bring broth to a boil and add tomatoes.
2. **Add Snails**
   Add snails and cook until they are tender, about 10 minutes.
3. **Prepare the Noodles**
   Cook rice vermicelli according to package instructions.
4. **Assemble the Dish**
   Place noodles in bowls, ladle broth and snails over, and garnish with fresh herbs.

Che Ba Mau (Three-Color Dessert)

Ingredients:

- 1/2 cup mung beans, soaked
- 1/2 cup red beans, cooked
- 1/2 cup green jelly (pandan flavored)
- Coconut milk
- Sugar to taste

Instructions:

1. **Prepare the Mung Beans**
   Cook mung beans until soft.
2. **Layer the Ingredients**
   In a glass, layer mung beans, red beans, and green jelly.
3. **Add Coconut Milk**
   Pour coconut milk over the layers and sweeten with sugar.
4. **Serve**
   Serve chilled or at room temperature.

Mi Quang with Shrimp

Ingredients:

- 200g rice noodles
- 300g shrimp, peeled and deveined
- 1 tablespoon turmeric powder
- 2 tablespoons fish sauce
- 1 onion, sliced
- 1 cup bean sprouts
- Fresh herbs for garnish
- Peanuts, crushed, for topping

Instructions:

1. **Marinate the Shrimp**
   Mix shrimp with turmeric and fish sauce. Set aside for 15 minutes.
2. **Cook the Noodles**
   Boil rice noodles according to package instructions, then drain and rinse.
3. **Sauté Onion and Shrimp**
   In a pan, sauté onion until translucent, add shrimp and cook until pink.
4. **Assemble the Dish**
   Place noodles in a bowl, top with shrimp, bean sprouts, and herbs. Garnish with crushed peanuts.

Bo La Lot (Beef Wrapped in Betel Leaves)

Ingredients:

- 500g ground beef
- 20 fresh betel leaves
- 2 tablespoons fish sauce
- 1 tablespoon sugar
- 1 tablespoon minced garlic
- Black pepper to taste

Instructions:

1. **Prepare the Filling**
   In a bowl, mix ground beef, fish sauce, sugar, garlic, and black pepper.
2. **Wrap the Beef**
   Take a betel leaf, place a spoonful of filling, and roll tightly.
3. **Grill the Rolls**
   Grill on medium heat until the beef is cooked through, about 10 minutes.
4. **Serve**
   Serve with rice and dipping sauce.

Banh Mi Thit Nuong (Grilled Pork Sandwich)

Ingredients:

- 1 baguette
- 300g grilled pork (thit nuong)
- 1 cucumber, sliced
- 1 carrot, pickled
- Fresh cilantro
- Mayonnaise or paté

Instructions:

1. **Prepare the Baguette**
   Slice the baguette lengthwise without cutting all the way through.
2. **Assemble the Sandwich**
   Spread mayonnaise or paté inside the baguette, add grilled pork, cucumber, pickled carrot, and cilantro.
3. **Serve**
   Cut into portions and serve fresh.

Hu Tieu Mi (Mixed Noodle Soup)

Ingredients:

- 200g egg noodles
- 200g shrimp, peeled
- 200g pork, thinly sliced
- 4 cups broth (chicken or pork)
- 1 onion, sliced
- Bean sprouts for garnish
- Fresh herbs for garnish

Instructions:

1. **Prepare the Broth**
   In a pot, bring broth to a boil and add onion.
2. **Cook the Noodles**
   Boil egg noodles according to package instructions, then drain.
3. **Add Proteins**
   Add shrimp and pork to the broth, cooking until done.
4. **Assemble the Soup**
   Place noodles in a bowl, pour broth with shrimp and pork over, and garnish with bean sprouts and herbs.

Cha Ca Thang Long (Dill Fish)

Ingredients:

- 300g fish fillets (white fish)
- 1/4 cup turmeric powder
- 1/4 cup fish sauce
- 1 cup fresh dill
- 1 onion, sliced
- 2 tablespoons peanuts, crushed

Instructions:

1. **Marinate the Fish**
   Mix fish with turmeric and fish sauce. Let marinate for 30 minutes.
2. **Cook the Fish**
   In a pan, sauté onion until soft, then add marinated fish and cook until flaky.
3. **Serve**
   Serve with dill and garnish with crushed peanuts.

Goi Muong (Green Mango Salad)

Ingredients:

- 2 green mangoes, julienned
- 1 carrot, julienned
- 1/2 cup roasted peanuts, crushed
- Fresh herbs (mint, cilantro)
- 2 tablespoons fish sauce
- 1 tablespoon lime juice
- 1 tablespoon sugar

Instructions:

1. **Prepare the Salad**
   In a bowl, combine green mango, carrot, peanuts, and herbs.
2. **Make the Dressing**
   Whisk together fish sauce, lime juice, and sugar.
3. **Toss and Serve**
   Pour dressing over salad, toss well, and serve chilled.

Banh Bao (Vietnamese Steamed Buns)

Ingredients:

- 2 cups all-purpose flour
- 1/2 cup sugar
- 1/2 cup warm water
- 1 teaspoon yeast
- 200g pork, diced
- 2 hard-boiled eggs, quartered
- 1 tablespoon soy sauce

Instructions:

1. **Make the Dough**
   Mix flour, sugar, yeast, and warm water until a dough forms. Knead and let rise for 1 hour.
2. **Prepare the Filling**
   In a bowl, mix pork with soy sauce.
3. **Shape the Buns**
   Divide dough into small balls, flatten, place filling and an egg quarter, then seal.
4. **Steam the Buns**
   Steam for 20 minutes until cooked through.

Thit Kho Tau (Braised Pork with Eggs)

Ingredients:

- 500g pork belly, cut into chunks
- 4 eggs, boiled and peeled
- 1/4 cup fish sauce
- 1/4 cup sugar
- 1 onion, sliced
- 2 cups coconut water

Instructions:

1. **Sear the Pork**
   In a pot, brown pork belly.
2. **Add Ingredients**
   Add onion, fish sauce, sugar, coconut water, and bring to a boil.
3. **Simmer**
   Add boiled eggs and simmer for about 40 minutes.
4. **Serve**
   Serve with rice.

Bun Chay (Vegetarian Noodles)

Ingredients:

- 200g rice noodles
- 1 cup mixed vegetables (carrots, bell peppers, and broccoli)
- 100g tofu, diced
- 2 tablespoons soy sauce
- 1 tablespoon sesame oil
- Fresh herbs for garnish (cilantro, mint)
- Crushed peanuts for topping

Instructions:

1. **Cook the Noodles**
   Boil the rice noodles according to package instructions, then drain and rinse.
2. **Stir-Fry the Vegetables and Tofu**
   In a pan, heat sesame oil, add tofu, and stir-fry until golden. Add mixed vegetables and soy sauce, cooking until tender.
3. **Assemble the Dish**
   Place noodles in a bowl, top with stir-fried vegetables and tofu, garnish with fresh herbs and crushed peanuts.

Ruou Vang (Vietnamese Wine Steamed Fish)

Ingredients:

- 500g whole fish (tilapia or snapper)
- 1 cup Vietnamese rice wine
- 1 tablespoon ginger, sliced
- 2 green onions, chopped
- 1 tablespoon soy sauce
- Fresh cilantro for garnish

Instructions:

1. **Prepare the Fish**
   Clean the fish and make diagonal slashes on both sides.
2. **Marinate**
   Rub the fish with ginger, soy sauce, and half of the green onions. Let marinate for 30 minutes.
3. **Steam the Fish**
   Place the fish in a steamer, pour rice wine over it, and steam for about 15-20 minutes until cooked through.
4. **Serve**
   Garnish with remaining green onions and cilantro before serving.

Xoi Ga (Sticky Rice with Chicken and Mushroom)

Ingredients:

- 2 cups glutinous rice
- 300g chicken thighs, diced
- 100g mushrooms, sliced
- 2 tablespoons soy sauce
- 1 tablespoon oyster sauce
- 2 tablespoons sesame oil
- Fried shallots for topping

Instructions:

1. **Prepare the Sticky Rice**
   Soak the glutinous rice in water for at least 4 hours, then steam for about 30 minutes until translucent.
2. **Cook the Chicken and Mushrooms**
   In a pan, heat sesame oil, add chicken, mushrooms, soy sauce, and oyster sauce, cooking until chicken is done.
3. **Assemble the Dish**
   Place sticky rice on a plate, top with chicken and mushroom mixture, and sprinkle with fried shallots before serving.

www.ingramcontent.com/pod-product-compliance
Lightning Source LLC
LaVergne TN
LVHW081501060526
838201LV00056BA/2873